A Note to Parents

DK READERS is a compelling program for beginning readers, designed in conjunction with leading literacy experts, including Dr. Linda Gambrell, Director of the Eugene T. Moore School of Education at Clemson University. Dr. Gambrell has served on the Board of Directors of the International Reading Association and as President of the National Reading Conference.

Beautiful illustrations and superb full-color photographs combine with engaging, easy-to-read stories to offer a fresh approach to each subject in the series. Each DK READER is guaranteed to capture a child's interest while developing his or her reading skills, general knowledge, and love of reading.

The five levels of DK READERS are aimed at different reading abilities, enabling you to choose the books that are exactly right for your child:

Pre-level 1: Learning to read
Level 1: Beginning to read
Level 2: Beginning to read alone
Level 3: Reading alone
Level 4: Proficient readers

The "normal" age at which a child begins to read can be anywhere from three to eight years old, so these levels are only a general guideline.

No matter which level you select, you can be sure that you are helping your child learn to read, then read to learn!

LONDON, NEW YORK, MUNICH,
MELBOURNE, AND DELHI

Art Editor Jacqueline Gooden
Series Editor Deborah Lock
Editorial Assistant Fleur Star
U.S. Editor Madeline Farbman
DTP Designer Almudena Díaz
Production Shivani Pandey
Picture Researcher
Sarah Stewart-Richardson
Illustrator Peter Dennis
Jacket Designer Chris Drew
Indexer Lynn Bresler

Consultant Aaron Murray

Reading Consultant
Linda Gambrell, Ph.D.

First American Edition, 2004
04 05 06 07 08 10 9 8 7 6 5 4 3 2 1
Published in the United States by DK Publishing, Inc.
375 Hudson Street, New York, New York 10014

Published in Great Britain by Dorling Kindersley Limited

A catalog record for this book is available
from the Library of Congress

ISBN 0-7566-0275-0 (pbk)
ISBN 0-7566-0276-9 (hbk)

Color reproduction by Colourscan, Singapore
Printed and bound in China by L Rex Printing Co., Ltd.

The publisher would like to thank the following
for their kind permission to reproduce their photographs:
POP=Popperfoto; CP=Camera Press; TRH=TRH Pictures;
IWM=Imperial War Museum; DDM=D-Day Museum, Portsmouth
Museum & Records Service; OSDDM=Ordnance Survey:
D-Day Museum, Portsmouth; DK=DK Images; KFSP=Katz/FSP
t=top; b=bottom; l=left; r=right
4-5 POP; 5 tr CP; 7 CP; 8 TRH: US National Archives; 9 Mary Evans
Picture Library; 10 TRH: USNA; 11 Hulton Archive/Getty Images;
12-13 TRH: US Navy; 14 DDM; 15 tr DDM;
15 b & 16 IWM; 17 t & b Public Record Office: The National
Archives Image Library; 18 IWM; 19 b IWM; 20 DK: Royal Signals
Museum; 21 t IWM; 21 b POP; 22-23 CP, 22 t POP; 23 r TRH:
US Navy; 25 b TRH; 26-27 t & b & 27 TRH: IWM; 28-29 Corbis:
Hulton-Deutsch Collection; 29 r Corbis: Michael St. Maur Sheil;
31 b CP; 32 t OSDDM; 35 b POP; 36-37 TRH: IWM; 36 t OSDDM;
37 t TRH: IWM; 37 b USNA; 38-39 TRH; 38 l CP: IWM;
39 b TRH; 40-41 CP: IWM, 40 t KFSP; 41 t POP, 41 b TRH;
42 t DK: IWM, 42 b POP; 43 t TRH: IWM, 43 b CP: IWM;
44 t IWM, 44 b POP; 45 TRH: DOD; 46-47 POP:
Mychele Daniau- AFP; 46 t KFSP: Stergiou Ioannis;
47 t KFSP: M. Lambert

All other images © Dorling Kindersley
For further information see: www.dkimages.com

Discover more at

www.dk.com

Contents

DK READERS

PROFICIENT 4 READERS

D-DAY
LANDINGS

The Story of the Allied Invasion

Written by Richard Platt

DK Publishing, Inc.

A hard life
Life in 1930s Germany was not easy. Germany had to pay for the damage from World War I. The people suffered as they did not have enough money to buy things. They even had to line up to get handouts of free food.

The world fights

At dawn on September 1, 1939, German tanks rumbled through the mist into Poland. Their invasion started World War II, which killed millions in land, sea, and air battles.

Germany's leader, Adolf Hitler, led his country into war to win back power, wealth, and land. Twenty years earlier, Germany had lost all of these after being defeated in World War I. The German people were poor and angry.

They believed that Hitler would give them a better life, and had elected him chancellor in 1933. He then began to build up Germany's military strength.

After the attack on Poland, the German army continued to invade other countries. By 1940, Hitler had conquered much of Europe.

A daring invasion by the Allied forces onto beaches in Normandy, France, on June 6, 1944—"D-day"—restarted the fight to push back the Germans.

Popular leader
In his speeches, Adolf Hitler promised that his Nazi party would make Germany strong and powerful, and restore the nation's pride.

German troops invading Poland.

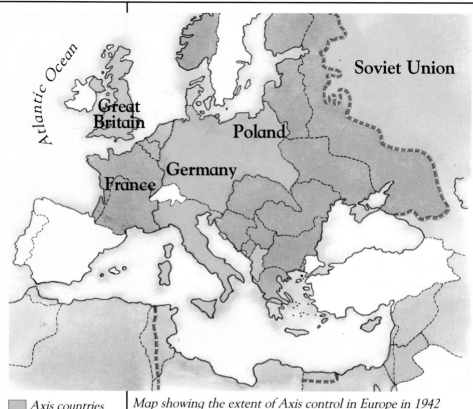

Map showing the extent of Axis control in Europe in 1942

Axis control
Germany invaded many countries in Europe from 1939 onward. Germany occupied France in 1942.

Germany did not fight alone. Hitler signed peace pacts with other countries around the world, including Japan. All these countries were called the "Axis."

When war began, France, Poland, and Great Britain fought the Axis powers, but later other nations helped. Together, the countries fighting the Axis were known as the "Allies."

The Soviet Union entered the war on the Axis side, but in June 1941, German forces invaded the country, breaking a peace pact between the two nations. After this, Soviet troops fought on the side of the Allies.

On December 7, 1941, a surprise Japanese attack on an American naval base at Pearl Harbor, Hawaii, led to the United States joining the Allied side.

Japan then went on to invade countries in Asia. War had spread across the whole world.

Soviet Union
In 1922, Russia and some neighboring countries formed the Soviet Union—the world's first communist state. They believed the workers should be in control, although this did not always happen. The 15 countries within the Union separated in 1991.

Destruction
More than 350 Japanese planes bombed Pearl Harbor. The devastating attack on battleships and the U.S. Navy yard lasted less than two hours, and 2,403 people died.

Franklin Roosevelt and Winston Churchill met several times during the war to discuss the possibility of an Allied attack into France. Three invasion plans were proposed, and, in 1943, they agreed upon Operation Overlord.

Roosevelt (left) talks to Churchill (right).

A plan to end the war

The Allies needed a great plan to win the war, so Britain's Prime Minister Winston Churchill went to the United States. There he held secret talks with President Franklin Delano Roosevelt.

They agreed that Allied troops would land in German-occupied France in the spring of 1944. This would lead to the recapture of Western Europe. The plan was code-named "Operation Overlord."

Great Britain

•Calais

English Channel

Seine Bay landing site

Normandy

R. Seine

Atlantic Ocean

France

Map of southern Britain and northern France

Where to land?
The town of Calais lies at the closest point of France to Britain, but the Allies did not choose it as their landing place. They thought it would be too obvious, and the Germans had the area well defended.

U.S. and British generals decided that the Seine Bay in Normandy, northern France, would be the best' place to land. It had good beaches for landing an army and its supplies. It was close to Britain, but was guarded by fewer German defenses than other places along the French coastline. Preparations for invasion began with the creation of maps and models of the area.

Making maps
Mapmakers took details from snapshots and postcards sent in by the British public from their vacations in Normandy before the war.

9

Life at camp
Ten soldiers shared each tent at a typical training camp. They were well fed to prepare them for the hardships ahead.

On Britain's south coast and in the countryside, soldiers secretly trained for the invasion of France. Nearly 3,500,000 of them gathered in huge camps that stretched for miles along the coastline. Ships constantly brought soldiers from the United States and Canada. Soon there were more American soldiers than British in southern England.

Under the command of the American General Dwight Eisenhower, the troops practiced crawling along flat sandy beaches and cutting barbed wire. They memorized maps and models of Normandy. They trained with new weapons, vehicles, and equipment until they could use them in the dark. But they were told very little about the invasion plans, so they could not pass on vital information to anyone else.

In command
General Dwight Eisenhower led Operation Overlord, with British General Bernard Montgomery in charge of the ground forces.

Eisenhower

Montgomery

To succeed, the invasion had to be a surprise attack, so a large number of soldiers had to travel to Normandy in one night. The Allies needed many ships and planes to do this, but they did not have enough metal to build them all.

The problem was solved by making thousands of wooden boats. They were flat-bottomed and could be sailed right onto the beaches.

Wooden gliders were also made. Towed by a powered plane and then released, they could glide down silently and land men far inland.

The glider's tow rope is attached to a plane.

The Allies also prepared for getting more supplies and troops across to France once the invasion had been successful. Liberating Europe could take many months.

Gliders
Despite being made of canvas and plywood, these gliders were strong enough to carry 15 men and a jeep.

CA1377

The fake invasion

Operation Overlord was a dangerous gamble. If Axis generals found out about the plan they would rush tanks to Normandy. With extra troops and guns there, they could stop the invasion.

To avoid a D-day disaster, the Allies decided to deceive Hitler with a plan they called "Operation Fortitude." They wanted him to think the Normandy landings were just a rehearsal. They pretended that a much bigger raid would come six weeks later at Calais—the point where France and England are closest.

The real plan had to be top secret, so people were kept away from the British coast where the troops were training, and the troops could not leave their camps.

14

The troops themselves were sworn to secrecy. Their letters home were censored to check that no one had accidentally written any important information about the invasion.

Operation Fortitude was a smart plan, but would it work?

Signs were put up warning people not to talk to the troops.

Training maps
Villages on the D-day landing site maps were called by other names to conceal the real location.

Campsites
The dummy camps were set up in Kent, which is the part of England nearest to France. The Germans would think this was the obvious place from which to start an invasion of Calais.

Bigbobs
Harbors were filled with dummy landing craft made from plywood and canvas.

The Germans would not be easy to fool. Their planes flew low over Britain taking pictures. If the trick was to work, it had to look as if the Allies really were getting ready to attack Calais.

In southeast England, where this imaginary attack would be launched, carpenters built 250 fake landing craft, called "Bigbobs." They floated them in rivers and at docks, and partly camouflaged them to give the impression that they were not meant to be seen.

Wooden tanks and trucks were positioned in fields. Seen from the air during the day, the tanks and trucks looked very real. Electricians wired lights in other fields. Germans flying over the area at night saw lights that gave the appearance of vast army camps.

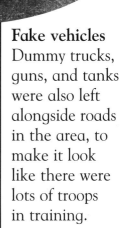

Fake vehicles
Dummy trucks, guns, and tanks were also left alongside roads in the area, to make it look like there were lots of troops in training.

To make the plan complete, the real invasion troops and ships farther west were hidden from view. Woodland areas and farms provided cover for the campsites. Camouflage netting was strung across the tops of the tents to blend in with the surrounding countryside.

Hidden among the trees, the real camps were not easy to spot from the air.

Bombs away!
The bombing campaign of spring 1944 lasted for three months, when 195,000 bombs were dropped. They destroyed bridges over the rivers in northern France, isolating the area from Axis reinforcements.

Allied planes bombing the beach forts near Calais

Airmen
Gunners on the planes had very dangerous jobs. They sat in glass turrets for a clear view of the skies while on the lookout for any enemy aircraft to shoot at. But from this position, they had little protection from enemy fire.

Allied bombers made the fake invasion plan look real by having a bombing campaign. Bombing always comes before big attacks. Road and railway bridges are hit to prevent extra troops from reaching the invasion site. Bombers pound radio stations and phone lines to stop news of the attack from spreading. These air attacks help an invasion succeed. However, they also help the enemy guess where troops will land.

To fool Axis generals, Allied planes bombed the beaches and key targets around Calais. Hitler thought that Calais was the main target of the Allied invasion, and kept many Axis troops stationed there for defense. Even after the D-day invasion began in Normandy, Hitler believed that a bigger attack would hit Calais. He thought Normandy was the fake invasion to draw his troops away from Calais, not the other way around.

"Hot bombs"
When dropped, the chemicals in these bombs would make a great heat to start fires.

Bomb damage
Churchill wanted to stop the bombing of Calais, which was devastated by the bombs.

Tuning in
During the war, national radio was used to broadcast coded messages, such as those hidden within poems.

Radio receiver
Radios used by spies had to be made small enough to fit inside everyday objects, such as suitcases.

The smartest part of Operation Fortitude was to let the Germans find out for themselves about the invasion so they would think it was real. Captured German spies were forced to report made-up rumors about the attack to their authorities.

Radio signals also spread false news. U.S. radio operators broadcasted from 22 dummy radio stations. They knew the Germans were listening and swapped bogus messages about training for a Calais invasion.

As the real invasion drew near, the Allies anxiously watched their enemies on the French coast, using radar to check the Axis location. To their relief, German commanders believed the spies' fake reports and the dummy army. They kept their troops around Calais and in nearby Holland.

What is radar?
Radar works by picking up signals sent out from huge radio masts. The signals bounce off aircraft and ships, revealing their positions.

The Axis also reinforced a line of defense called the Atlantic Wall, which ran along the coast from France to Holland. The strongest point was at Calais. The deception had worked!

The Atlantic Wall
The coastal defense wall, built in 1942, included gun forts, and land and sea mines to stop Allied troops from crossing the English Channel.

Radar operators tracked the movements of enemy ships and planes.

Attack!

On Friday, June 2, 1944, transport ships set off across the English Channel with 170,000 soldiers aboard. "Operation Neptune" had begun. Supply ships and tugs towing artificial docks joined the fleet. Then, on Saturday, near-disaster struck. A storm was forecast that would swamp the landing craft and affect the bombing raids.

Neptune
The first phase of Operation Overlord—to invade Normandy—was code-named Neptune, after the Roman god of the ocean.

General Eisenhower decided the invasion must wait. The huge fleet carried the seasick troops back to England.

On Monday, June 5, Eisenhower met his generals again. If the troops did not leave soon, they would have to cancel the attack. Just in time, the weather forecast changed.

"OK," ordered Eisenhower. "We'll go!"

Once the ships had set sail again for France, the airborne troops took off, flying swiftly over southern England. It was the largest air fleet ever assembled in one place.

Seasickness
Flat-bottomed boats caused many troops to be seasick. The boats bounced up and down as they sat on the waves, rather than cutting through them.

Date of attack
Until the generals decided when to launch the attack, the invasion date was unknown; so during the planning stages it was referred to as D-day in which "D" stands for the word "day."

Paratroopers
These troops are trained to use parachutes, and are dropped into the battle zone behind enemy lines. For D-day, the paratroopers had guns that dismantled into three parts, which were placed in a bag for the jump.

The first Allies to reach Normandy soon after midnight on Tuesday, June 6, were paratroopers and glider crews. Enemy guns on the ground shot down many of the Allied aircraft. Pilots lost their way in the low clouds, and some gliders crash-landed in fields and rivers. Paratroopers ended up miles from their buddies, stumbling around in the dark.

Using children's clicker toys, the troops were able to signal their position. Despite the confusion, enough of them met up and attacked enemy strongholds. They took over vital bridges, and captured four raised roads for safe crossing over flooded land.

Clicker toys
All troops were given metal toys, which clicked like a cricket's noise when squeezed.

Meanwhile, Allied bomber aircraft started their attack, heading for Caen. Their mission was to destroy the big guns inside concrete forts near the beach. The attack started at midnight, with 3,500 heavy bombers flying high over Normandy's coastline. But clouds hid many of the targets and half the planes flew home without dropping a single bomb.

Caen
The town of Caen was the ancient capital of Normandy. As the major town near the Seine Bay, it was a key target for the Allies.

The next wave of 1,700 light bombers had better luck. They flew in low just before dawn. Their bombs helped destroy the forts.

Finally, three dozen battleships positioned along the coast took over. Huge guns on their decks pounded the beaches and forts with shells. The noise was tremendous and the air was filled with thick, yellow smoke. The power of the guns made the ships shake and creak. Any troops standing on deck were covered in heavy dust.

The bombing and shelling stopped just as the sun rose. The attack lasted just over six hours. In the eerie silence that followed, the troop invasion began.

Bombers
Heavy bomber planes could carry up to 14,000 lb (6,342 kg) of bombs. The light bombers included the *Mosquito,* a fast flyer that was mostly made from wood.

Dazzling
Battleships were painted in a mix of colors, called "dazzle" patterns, that made it hard for the enemy to judge how far away they were.

D-day beaches
Code names were given to each of the D-day landing areas. They were Utah, Omaha, Gold, Juno, and Sword.

In the early morning light, landing craft surged from the sea on the west of the Seine Bay. They headed for the beach code-named "Utah." This was one of two places where the U.S. troops would land.

At "H-hour," U.S. soldiers waded from their landing craft without firing a shot. There was no need to. Only a single, big enemy gun protected the beach, but it was silent. Shells fired from the battleships had damaged it, and the German soldiers at the fort surrendered.

When the troops got ashore they had a surprise. A current had washed them down the coast. They were a mile (1.6 kilometers) from where they had planned to land! It was a lucky mistake, for there were fewer defenses here than anywhere else on the Normandy coast.

Flooding fields
The fields around Utah beach were flooded by the River Douve. German leaders kept the river's locks open to make sure the land was well flooded. They thought that the Allied troops would not be able to cross the flooded land.

The Americans soon found out why there were hardly any enemy troops and guns defending the beach. Swamps and flooded fields covered the area and made a natural defense against invasion. Some soldiers moved inland along a raised road that stood high and dry above the water. The rest waded to higher ground, holding their guns above their heads to keep them dry.

Behind them, engineers and the Navy demolition units quickly came ashore to carry out their work.

They carefully destroyed the land mines and any other obstacles that were buried on the beach.

When the beach was clear, more troops, tanks, and other vehicles came ashore safely.

By nightfall, 23,000 men and 1,700 vehicles had landed with only a few casualties reported. If every beach was like Utah, the invasion would be like a training exercise.

Clearing mines
Engineers used hand probes and electronic detectors to find the buried mines. Then they detonated the mines in controlled explosions.

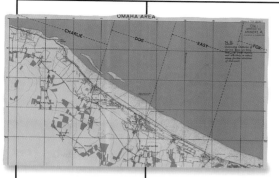

Omaha
Omaha beach stretched for over 6 miles (10 kilometers). To make the invasion easier, the beach was divided into four sections, as shown on the training map above.

"Omaha" beach, just 15 miles (24 kilometers) away, was harder to capture. There were cliffs more than 100 feet (30 meters) high towering over the beach. From there, German defenders had 100 big guns pointing at the shore. Aerial bombardments had failed to destroy them. Allied tanks were now supposed to lead the attack on them. However, before the tanks could land, waves swamped them.

Bullets ripped into the U.S. troops wading through the shallow water. Shells exploded all around them. Soldiers were weighed down by the heavy loads in their packs. If they fell over, they were unable to get up, and drowned. Those who reached the beach took cover in the surf, or under the seawall.

Once ashore, they faced mines, barbed wire, the high cliffs, and more bullets. Within minutes of when the attack began, the surf and sand were red with blood.

Cliff defenses
Omaha was the most heavily defended D-day beach. Coastal cliffs provided a natural lookout post for Axis troops.

Obstacles
Some U.S. troops took shelter behind the beach obstacles that were designed to stop the Allied landing craft from reaching the shore.

33

More and more soldiers poured onto the beach, advancing toward the cliffs. There were five exits from the beach, but the Germans had them covered. Some troops were hidden from enemy fire by smoke from burning grass. A few brave men risked almost certain death to throw grenades into the German fortifications known as pill boxes. Battleships close to the shore shelled other forts, destroying their guns. Little by little, small groups of soldiers fought their way through the German defenses. By noon, the American troops were beginning to win the battle.

When the sun set on D-day, 3,000 American soldiers lay dead, but "bloody Omaha" beach had been captured. The U.S. troops could advance into France.

Grenades
Troops using time-delay grenades had up to six seconds to throw the grenade once its safety pin was released.

Pill boxes
The small, concrete gun shelters were named after the shape and size of the tiny boxes in which pills are kept.

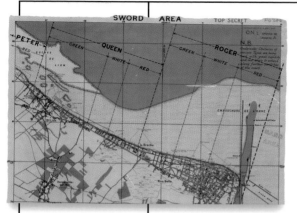

To the east of the Seine Bay, British and Canadian troops poured onto the beaches code-named "Gold," "Juno," and "Sword." Special tanks had cleared safe paths through the mines and the mud on the beaches.

Beach maps
It took months to check out each D-day landing site. Training maps gave details of the land and any dangers that the troops might find.

Bobbins
These tanks laid strong matting over the mud to make instant roads for the troops to use.

Tanks named "Crabs" whirled chains to set off mines.

Battleships and bombers had destroyed most of the big guns aimed at the coast. The beaches were too wide for the few Axis troops posted there to defend. Many were Soviet and Polish soldiers who had been forced into the German army. They tried to fight the Allies at first, but soon surrendered. There were few British casualties at Gold beach, but at Juno beach the Canadians did not have such an easy time. Their landing craft became tangled in iron posts planted in the sand.

Funny tanks
Special tanks, such as Bobbins and Crabs, were nicknamed "Funnies."

Lots of uses
Bridge-laying tanks spanned wide gaps. Other Funnies were used to smash concrete defenses, or shine bright lights to blind the enemy.

Sword beach
At only 3 miles (5 kilometers) long, Sword beach was the smallest invasion site. Fewer troops landed here than at the other beaches, but they had less time to clear the beach of obstacles as heavy winds were pushing the tide in.

Cherbourg
The Allies needed to capture a large port from which they could land backup troops and supplies. Cherbourg was the ideal place on the tip of Normandy.

At Sword beach, German guns sprayed the beach with bullets. It was captured by the British troops only after three hours of fighting.

German tanks from Caen tried to stop the British advance, but there were too few of them. Hitler still believed the big invasion would come at Calais, and he was slow to order extra German tanks to move into Normandy.

When the order came, it was too late. Allied troops had taken the coast, and were pushing inland.

Each of the five beach invasions had its own target site to capture. Utah beach was near Cherbourg port. Behind Juno beach was an airfield. Troops at Omaha and Sword beaches aimed for Caen.

The troops from Gold beach took control of a major road junction. They were in the middle of the five beaches, so they provided a contact point between all the troops.

Panzer tanks
The German tank unit was called *Panzer*, which means "armor."

German Panzer tanks were overwhelmed.

Getting the first troops ashore on D-day was just the start of the invasion. Winning control of Europe would take much longer. So, on the shores of Normandy, the Allies landed more troops, and built artificial docks called Mulberry harbors, made from huge concrete blocks that were sunk to the seabed.

Mulberries
Parts for the two Mulberry harbors were secretly made in Britain. They were then used at Omaha and Gold beaches.

Floating roadways joined the unloading platforms to the beach.

Inside these docks, seven cargo ships could safely unload their supplies at the same time. The army's daily rations of food, bullets, and other supplies filled 520 large trucks. The whole operation was like shifting a city to France, and keeping it moving.

Large amounts of fuel were needed. It took 168 gallons (635 liters) of gasoline to fill some battle tanks. A pipeline laid along the seabed supplied fuel from England to France. As the troops advanced through France, they laid temporary pipelines, which were supplied by tanker ships off the coast of Normandy.

Daily rations
Each soldier's food rations included canned meat, cookies, coffee, and chewing gum.

Oil pipelines
The secret plan to lay a pipeline along the sea-bed was called PLUTO—"Pipe Line Under The Ocean."

Winning the war

In the weeks after D-day, Allied soldiers and airmen fought bravely to capture towns and ports. During July, they freed Normandy.

Eighty thousand U.S. troops landed near Cannes in the south of France for "Operation Anvil." Together with the D-day troops, they stormed across France, helped by the Resistance— French people who had formed secret groups after Germany defeated France in 1940. They became spies for the Allies, passing on information about German defenses in France, and sabotaging Axis communications. Since D-day, they had been launching surprise attacks on German forces all over the country.

French Forces (FFI)
The FFI was set up by General Charles de Gaulle to unite the Resistance groups in France.

Operation Anvil
A successful landing in the south of France gave the Allies another port, and drew Axis defenses away from Normandy.

On August 19, 1944, Resistance fighters in Paris rose up against the German authorities. A week later French and U.S. troops recaptured the capital. Around the same time, other Allied troops had liberated cities in Italy and Belgium. The German stronghold in Europe was weakening. Now nothing could stop the Allied advance on Germany!

French Resistance About two-thirds of the Resistance supported de Gaulle's FFI. The rest were members of communist fighting groups.

The people of Paris lined the streets to cheer and thank the Allied troops as they entered the city.

Germany took much longer to defeat. American and British troops advanced from the west across the River Rhine. The Soviet army moved toward the German capital, Berlin, from the east through Hungary and Austria. Allied bombers pounded German cities from above. Finally, in April 1945, Soviet troops surrounded Berlin, and a week later they entered the city. On May 7, 1945, Germany surrendered, and the next day the Allied nations celebrated their victory in Europe— "VE day."

Berlin falls
On May 2, 1945, a Soviet soldier waved his nation's flag from the roof of the ruined Reichstag— the German parliament building in Berlin.

Hitler's bunker
Hitler is believed to have killed himself in his Berlin bunker just before the Allies entered the city.

The war in the Pacific continued. Since 1942, Japan had invaded many countries in the Pacific. The U.S. had battled to stop Japan's expansion. By 1945, Japan's Navy and air force were weakening under U.S. attack, but Japan's leaders would not surrender. So in early August, the Allies dropped atomic bombs on two Japanese cities, Hiroshima and Nagasaki. Hundreds of thousands of people died.

The deadly power of these weapons forced the Japanese emperor to finally accept defeat. He surrendered on September 2, 1945.

Pacific battles
In 1942, the U.S. Navy defeated Japan at the Battle of Coral Sea. It was a turning point for the war in the Pacific, stopping Japan from invading Australia.

Atomic bomb
A team of scientists based in New Mexico developed the atomic bomb in 1945.

Japan's formal surrender took place aboard the USS Missouri.

Reminders
Sections of the Mulberry harbors can still be seen at Arromanches—the site of Gold beach in Normandy.

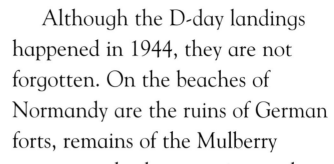

Overlord Arch
The U.S. National D-day Memorial—a triumphal arch—is located in Bedford, Virginia. The town lost the most casualties for the size of its population on D-day. The arch was built 44 ft 6 in (13.5 meters) tall to remind people of the date of D-day—June 6, 1944.

Although the D-day landings happened in 1944, they are not forgotten. On the beaches of Normandy are the ruins of German forts, remains of the Mulberry harbors, rusting tanks, and silent guns. Nearby, long rows of white crosses mark the graves of the 4,500 Allied soldiers who died on D-day.

War museums in Normandy and around the world recreate the dramatic events using the soldiers' belongings and personal stories. The nations involved in the D-day landings have built their own memorials for the troops they lost.

On special anniversaries, D-day parades and events are held. Veterans who fought on the beaches that day return to join the commemorations and remember the people who helped liberate Europe.

With thanks
Crowds cheered the troops at the 40th anniversary parade held in France.

D-day veterans visit the war graves in France.

Glossary

Allies
One of the two groups of countries that fought in World War II, including the U.S., Britain, and Canada.

Atomic bombs
Hugely powerful bombs that cause sickness and death from radiation poisoning long after they explode.

Axis
One of the two groups of countries that fought in World War II, led by Germany and Italy.

Bombers
Large aircraft designed to drop bombs on the enemy.

Bunker
A strong, small fortress, often built under the ground as a shelter from aerial bombardment.

Commemorations
Ceremonies to remember events from the past.

Detonate
To set off or explode, usually a bomb.

Fortifications
Defenses including concrete forts, pill boxes, and other strong buildings built to defend a position.

Gliders
Aircraft that fly without an engine.

Grenades
Small bombs, thrown by hand.

Harbors
Ports or coastal areas protected from wind and waves, where ships can tie up to load or unload.

Invasion
The movement of a country's soldiers across the border of another country, aiming to capture it.

Landing craft
Flat-bottomed boats that can sail into shallow water to land troops on beaches.

Mines
Buried bombs triggered to explode when vehicles or people pass over them.

Neutral
A country or person that is not a member of either side in a conflict.

Operation Fortitude
The code name for the plans to deceive Hitler about the date and landing site of the D-day invasion.

Operation Neptune
The code name for the first phase of Operation Overlord that involved the invasion of Normandy.

Operation Overlord
The code name for the Allied plan to invade France and recapture Western Europe.

Peace pact
An agreement between two warring nations to stop the fighting.

Rations
Food supplies that are shared out in small amounts.

Sabotage
To destroy something on purpose.

Seawall
A strong wall on a coast, built to stop waves from wearing away the land.

Shells
Bombs fired from large guns.

Shrapnel
The deadly pieces of metal from exploding shells and bombs.

Spies
People who disguise their identity so that they can enter enemy land and discover war secrets.

Stronghold
Any place that is safe from attack because of its position or strong walls.

Troops
Groups of soldiers.